MEET THE ROYALS

Dukes

Enslow Publishing
101 W. 23rd Street
Suite 240
New York, NY 10011
USA

enslow.com

Sarita McDaniel

charity A group that helps people in need.

duchy An area ruled by a duke or duchess.

duke A male royal who runs a duchy.

kingdom The area ruled by a monarch.

monarch A king or queen.

prime minister A person who is chosen by the people to make decisions for a country.

royal A king or queen; a person who is in the king or queen's family.

Contents

Words to Know 2

What Is a Monarchy? 5

The Royal Family 7

Who's in Charge? 9

A Duke's Job 11

The Last Grand Duke 13

Royal Dukes 15

A Queen and a Duke? 17

A Wedding Gift 19

Changing Roles 21

Friendship Between
Countries 23

Learn More 24

Index 24

There have been many famous monarchs. This photo shows the Romanovs, a royal family from Russia.

What Is a Monarchy?

Some countries have a king or queen. That person is called a **monarch**. The job of king or queen usually passes from parent to child.

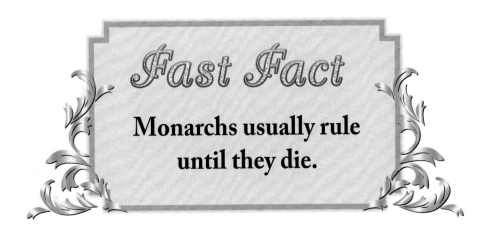

Fast Fact

Monarchs usually rule until they die.

This photo of the British royal
family includes the queen, princes,
princesses, dukes, and duchesses.

THE ROYAL FAMILY

The family of the king or queen is called the **royal** family. Each family member has a title. These may include prince, princess, **duke**, and duchess.

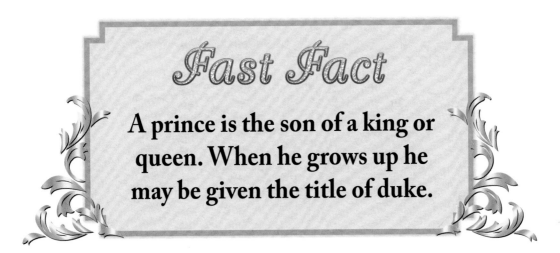

Fast Fact

A prince is the son of a king or queen. When he grows up he may be given the title of duke.

Alnwick Castle is the home of the Duke of Northumberland in England.

WHO'S IN CHARGE?

Kings and queens rule over large **kingdoms**.

Duchies are smaller parts of the kingdom.

A man who rules a duchy is called a duke.

Fast Fact

The wife of a duke is
called a duchess.

This painting shows a king on his throne in 1715. It was the duke's job to help the king.

A Duke's Job

The duke can help carry out the king's orders. He may also look after the people who live in his duchy. But some dukes do not have a duchy. They are a duke in name only.

Fast Fact

The duke's title includes the name of an area. Britain's Prince William is Duke of Cambridge.

Henri, Grand Duke of Luxembourg, stands with his wife and five children.

THE LAST GRAND DUKE

Luxembourg is the only duchy still ruled by a duke.

His name is Henri, Grand Duke of Luxembourg.

He shares power with the **prime minister**.

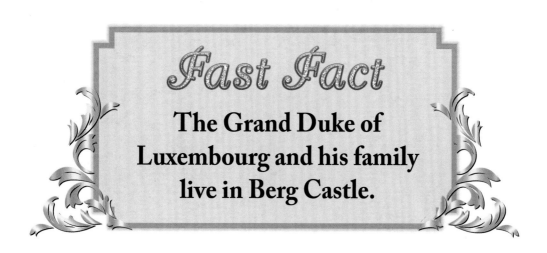

Fast Fact

The Grand Duke of Luxembourg and his family live in Berg Castle.

British princes William and Harry are also both dukes.

ROYAL DUKES

Some princes are also dukes. When a duke is related to the king, he is called a royal duke. Some kings are also dukes.

Fast Fact

Dukes are addressed as "Your Grace." Royal dukes are addressed as "Your Royal Highness."

Queen Elizabeth II has many titles.
She is a duke as well as a lord.

A Queen and a Duke?

Men usually hold the title of duke. But Queen Elizabeth II is also a duke. She is Duke of Normandy and Duke of Lancaster in Lancashire.

Fast Fact

Duke is the highest royal title after king or queen.

The Duke of Edinburgh wears a coronet at the coronation of Queen Elizabeth II.

A WEDDING GIFT

In the United Kingdom, a prince may receive the title of duke as a wedding gift. When Prince Harry married Meghan Markle, he was named the Duke of Sussex.

Fast Fact

A duke wears a crown called a coronet.

The Duke of Cambridge visits with an ambulance **charity**.

CHANGING ROLES

Today most royal dukes do not make decisions for the country. But they play an important role everywhere they go. They are a symbol of the royal family. They work with charities to help others.

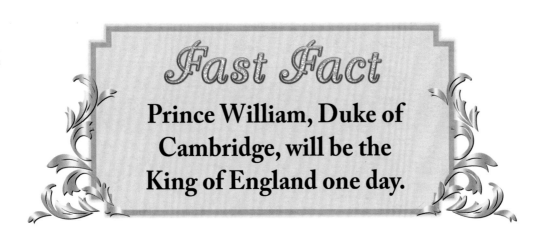

Fast Fact

Prince William, Duke of Cambridge, will be the King of England one day.

**Grand Duke Henri of Luxembourg
meets with the president of Vietnam.**

FRIENDSHIP BETWEEN COUNTRIES

A modern duke travels a lot. He goes to important events in his country. He travels around the world. He meets with world leaders. It is a sign of friendship between countries.

Fast Fact

A duke must study the local customs of every country he visits.

LEARN MORE

BOOKS

DK. *Castles*. New York, NY: DK, 2019.

Gagne, Tammy. *Prince Harry*. Hallandale, FL: Mitchell Lane, 2018.

Zeiger, Jennifer. *Queen Elizabeth II*. Chicago, IL: Children's Press, 2015.

WEBSITES

DK Find Out Kings and Queens
dkfindout.com/us/history/kings-and-queens/
Learn more about monarchs throughout history.

The Home of the Royal Family
royal.uk
Find out more about the British royal family.

INDEX

coronet, 19
duchess, 6, 7, 9
duchy, 9, 11, 13
king, 5, 7, 9, 10, 15, 17

Luxembourg, 12, 13, 22
prince, 6, 7, 19
Prince Harry, 14, 19

Prince William, 11, 14, 20, 21
princess, 6, 7
queen, 5, 6, 7, 9

royal duke, 15,
royal family, 4, 7

Published in 2020 by Enslow Publishing, LLC
101 W. 23rd Street, Suite 240, New York, NY 10011

Copyright © 2020 by Enslow Publishing, LLC

Library of Congress Cataloging-in-Publication Data

Names: McDaniel, Sarita, author.
Title: Dukes / Sarita McDaniel.
Description: New York : Enslow Publishing, 2020. | Series: Meet the royals | Includes bibliographical references and index. | Audience: K to grade 3.
Identifiers: LCCN 2019008578| ISBN 9781978511958 (library bound) | ISBN 9781978511934 (pbk.) | ISBN 9781978511941 (6 pack)
Subjects: LCSH: Monarchy—Juvenile literature. | Kings and rulers—Juvenile literature.
Classification: LCC JC375 .S265 2020 | DDC 321/.6—dc23

LC record available at https://lccn.loc.gov/2019008578

Printed in the United States of America

To Our Readers: We have done our best to make sure all websit addresses in this book were active and appropriate when we went press. However, the author and the publisher have no control ov and assume no liability for the material available on those websit or on any websites they may link to. Any comments or suggestio can be sent by e-mail to customerservice@enslow.com.

Photo Credits: Dukes – Research by Bruce Donnola
Cover, p. 1 DEA Picture Library/De Agostini Picture Librar Getty Images; p. 4 Everett Historical/Shutterstock.com; p. 6 © A Images; p. 8 iLongLoveKing/Shutterstock.com; p. 10 adoc-phot Corbis Historical/Getty Images; p. 12 Raymond Reuter/Sygm Getty Images; p. 14 Samir Hussein/WireImage/Getty Images; 16 Stuart C. Wilson/Getty Images; p. 18 ZUMA Press, Inc./Alar Stock Photo; p. 20 WPA Pool/Getty Images; p. 22 Hoang Di Nam/AFP/Getty Images; cover, p. 1 (background), interior pag (borders) Alona Syplyak/Shutterstock.com, cover and inter pages (decorative motifs) View Pixel/Shutterstock.com